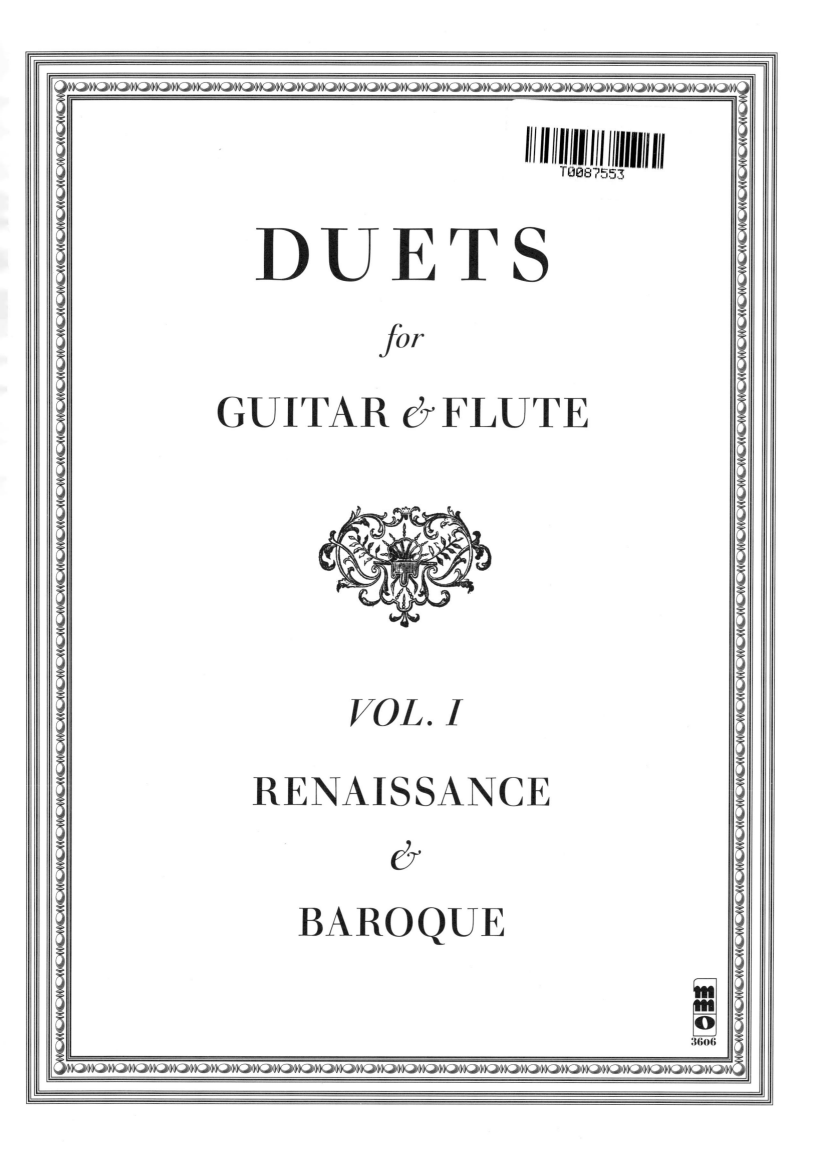

DUETS

for

GUITAR & FLUTE

VOL. I

RENAISSANCE

&

BAROQUE

mmo
3606

SUGGESTIONS FOR USING THIS MMO EDITION

*W*E HAVE TRIED to create a product that will provide you an easy way to learn and perform these duets with a complete accompaniment in the comfort of your own home. Because it involves a fixed accompaniment performance, there is an inherent lack of flexibility in tempo. The following MMO features and techniques will reduce these inflexibilities and help you maximize the effectiveness of the MMO practice and performance system:

We have observed generally accepted tempi, but some may wish to perform at a different tempo, or to slow down or speed up the accompaniment for practice purposes. You can purchase from MMO (or from other audio and electronics dealers) specialized CD players and recorders which allow variable speed while maintaining proper pitch. This is an indispensable tool for the serious musician and you may wish to look into purchasing this useful piece of equipment for full enjoyment of all your MMO editions.

Where the performer begins a piece *solo* or without an introduction from the accompanying instrument, we have provided a set of subtle taps before each piece as appropriate to help you enter with the proper tempo.

We want to provide you with the most useful practice and performance accompaniments possible. If you have any suggestions for improving the MMO system, please feel free to contact us. You can reach us by e-mail at *mmogroup@musicminusone.com*.

A NOTE ABOUT THE 'PRACTICE TEMPO' DISC

*a*s an aid during the early stages of learning these pieces, we have created a second 'practice tempo' compact disc which contains accompaniments which have been slowed by approximately 20%. This will allow you to begin at a comfortably reduced speed until fingerings and technique are more firmly in grasp, at which time the full-speed disc can be substituted.

mmo
3606

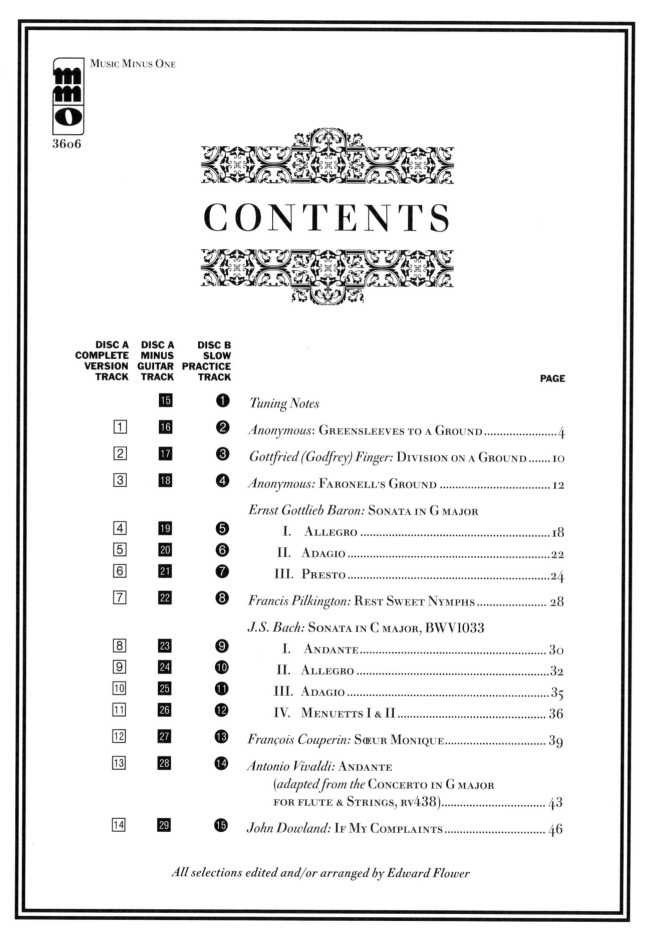

CONTENTS

All selections edited and/or arranged by Edward Flower

GREENSLEEVES TO A GROUND

Anonymous

One measure of taps (two taps) precedes music

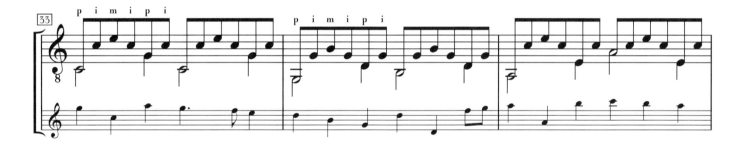

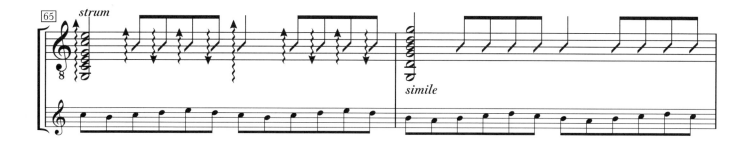

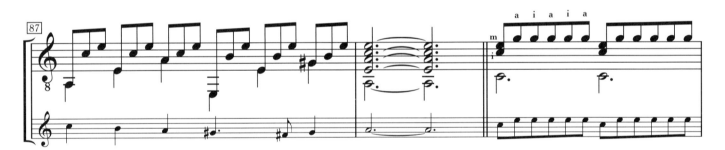

DIVISION ON A GROUND

Gottfried (Godfrey) Finger
(1660-1723)

One measure of taps (4 taps) precedes music

FARONELL'S GROUND

Guitar: capo to 3rd. fret.

Anonymous

Two measures of taps (6 taps) precedes music

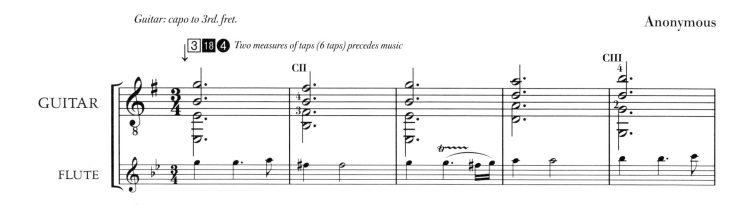

SONATE
G MAJOR 𝄞 G-DUR

Ernst Gottlieb Baron
(1696-1760)

Two measures of taps (4 taps) precede music

Allegro

GUITAR

FLUTE

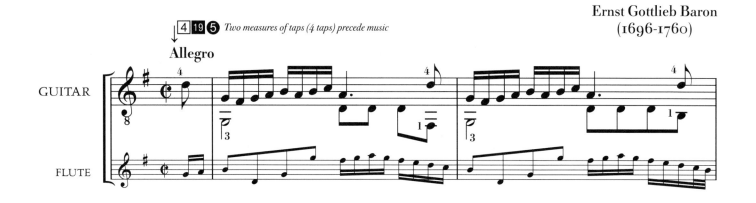

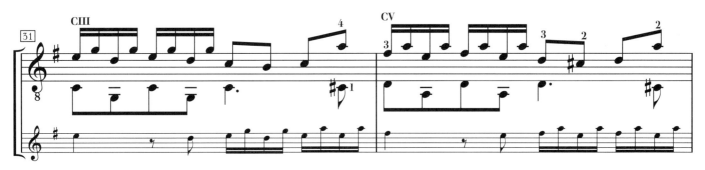

II.

III.

6 21 7 *Two measures of taps (4 taps) precede music*

Presto

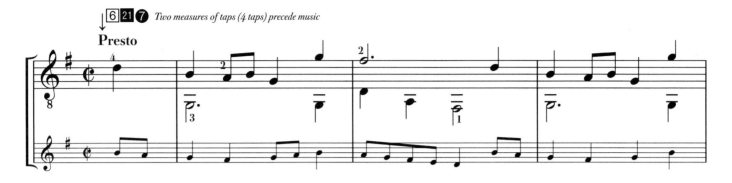

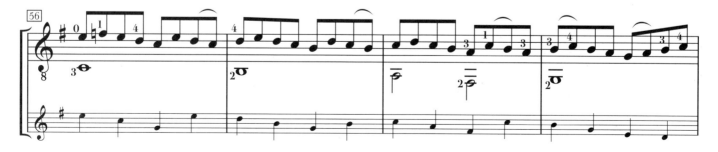

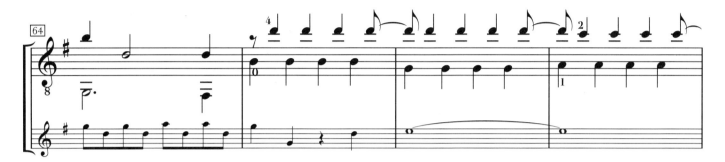

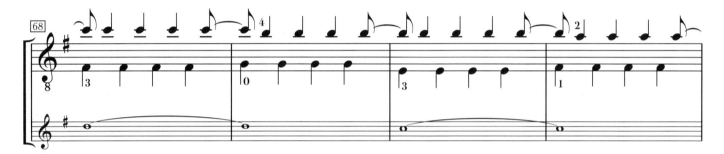

REST SWEET NYMPHS

Francis Pilkington
(1565-1638)

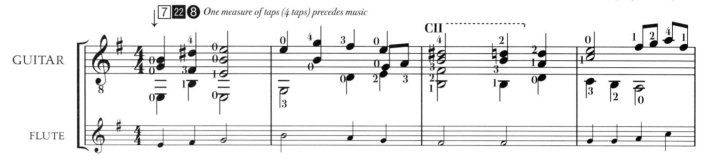

*)N.B.

*) this is an example of free ornamentation in the flute part

SONATE
C MAJOR ♪ C DUR
BWV 1033

I.

Johann Sebastian Bach
(1685-1750)

8 23 9 *One measure of taps (4 taps) precedes music*

Andante

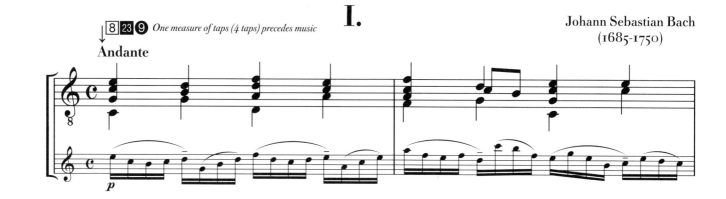

CIII   **Presto**

II.

9 24 10 *One measure of taps (3 taps) precedes music*

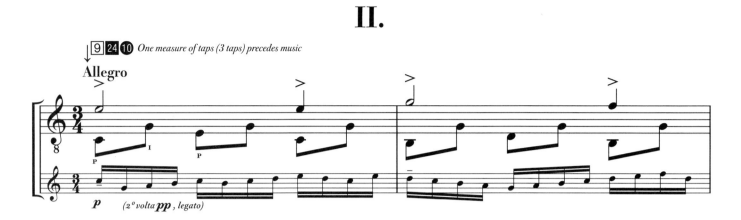

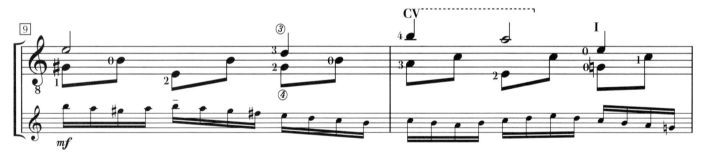

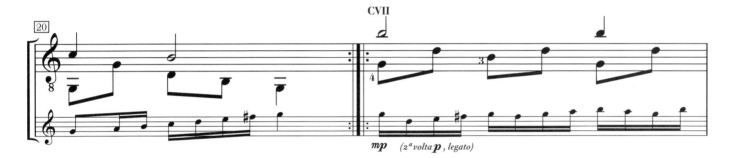

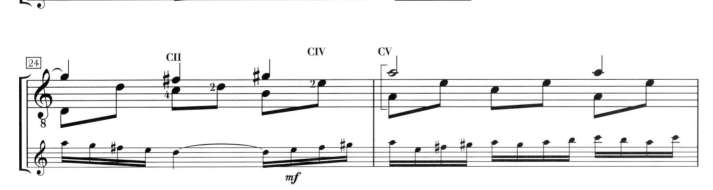

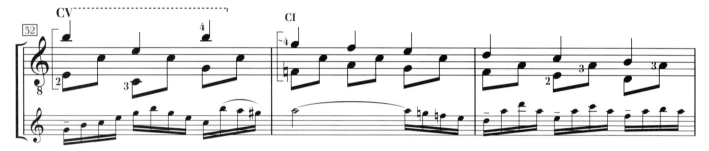

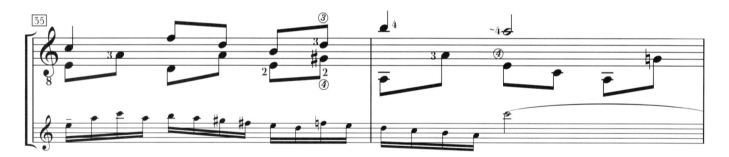

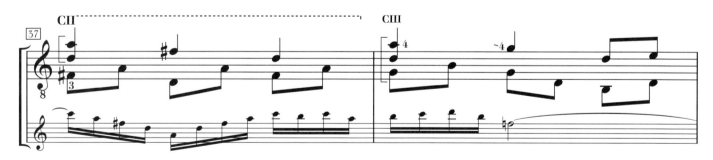

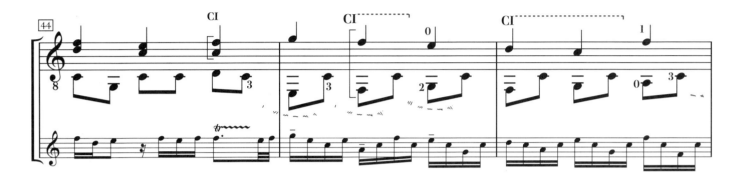

III.

11 25 12 *½ measure of taps (4 taps) precedes music*

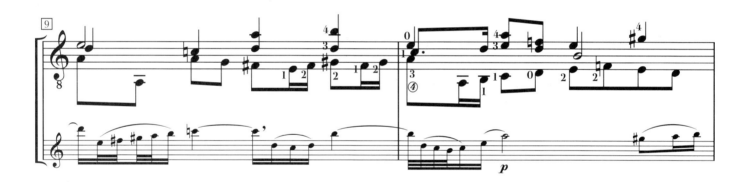

IV.

Menuett I

Menuett II

Da Capo
Menuett I

SŒUR MONIQUE

François Couperin
(1668-1773)

ANDANTE
adapted from the
CONCERTO *in* G MAJOR
for FLUTE & STRINGS, RV438

Antonio Vivaldi
(1685-1741)

GUITAR

FLUTE

IF MY COMPLAINTS

John Dowland
(1563-1626)

Engraving: Wieslaw Novak

MMO 3606

MUSIC MINUS ONE
50 Executive Boulevard
Elmsford, New York 10523-1325
800.669.7464 U.S. ← 914.592.1188 International

www.musicminusone.com
mmogroup@musicminusone.com

MMO 3606

Printed in Canada